✇ **W9-BQX-939**

HandsOnPsych, Version 2.0

Pearson Education Canada's
Interactive Modules for Psychology

CD-ROM for Windows® and Macintosh®

Tom Harrigan
Red River College

Department of Psychology
University of Manitoba

PEARSON
Prentice
Hall

Toronto

For technical support of this product, please call 416-386-3413 or email webinfo.pub-canada@pearsoned.com

National Library of Canada Cataloguing in Publication

Harrigan, Tom, 1964–
    HandsOnPsych, version 2.0 : Pearson Education Canada's interactive modules for psychology / Tom Harrigan.

Accompanied by CD-ROM.
Previously published under title: MyPsychLab.
ISBN 0-13-121719-4

1. Psychology. I. Harrigan, Tom, 1964– . MyPsychLab. II. Title. III. Title: Hands on psych.

BF79.H37 2005   150   C2004-900269-4

Copyright © 2005, 2003 Pearson Education Canada Inc., Toronto, Ontario.

Pearson Prentice Hall. All rights reserved. This publication is protected by copyright and permission should be obtained from the publisher prior to any prohibited reproduction, storage in a retrieval system, or transmission in any form or by any means, electronic, mechanical, photocopying, recording, or likewise. For information regarding permission, write to the Permissions Department.

This edition is for sale in Canada only.

ISBN 0-13-121719-4

Vice President, Editorial Director: Michael J. Young
Acquisitions Editor: Ky Pruesse
Executive Marketing Manager: Judith Allen
Senior Media Editor: Matthew Christian
Production Editor: Söğüt Y. Güleç
Copy Editor: Dana Kahan
Proofreaders: Lisa Berland, Trish O'Reilly, Katie Shafley
Production Coordinator: Patricia Ciardullo
Manager, New Media and Editorial Services: David Jolliffe
Senior Online Resources Developer: Robin Blair
New Media Work: Dalton Miller
Page Layout: Phyllis Seto
Permissions and Photo Research: Sandy Cooke
Cover and Interior Design (booklet): Alex Li, Miguel Acevedo
Cover Image: Comstock Production Department

2 3 4 5   09 08 07 06 05

Printed and bound in Canada.

Contents

Welcome

Dear Student,

Welcome to *HandsOnPsychology*. It seems like only yesterday when the Psychology Department at the University of Manitoba, Pearson Education Canada, and I began working on the goal of creating ten fun, informative, and stimulating psychology modules, where the dizzying language and theories presented in the classroom could become personal, real, and concrete. The first ten modules were so well received by your predecessors that we decided to enhance the existing modules, based on the comments and experiences of many users, and create a few more—we now have 16 of them.

Each module encourages your learning by using the latest digital technology to create a variety of learning environments. Within each module you'll find clear objectives, descriptive notes on specific classroom topics, cartoons and illustrations, a glossary, pop-up questions, video and audio clips, weblinks, games, interactive activities, crosswords, and lots of practice tests—all packaged into manageable units designed to complement your professor's lectures, bring psychological theories to life, and hopefully improve your grades!

We had a blast creating these modules and we hope you find them fun, informative, and useful tools in your pursuit of psychological knowledge and understanding.

Tom Harrigan

An Introduction to *HandsOnPsych*

With this innovative learning tool, *HandsOnPsych* CD-ROM, Version 2.0, you can actively explore and master the core topics commonly included in introductory psychology courses. Each of the modules combines a range of learning opportunities and experiences within a well paced, pedagogically sound framework that reinforces and consolidates concepts in a stimulating and exciting way. Navigation within and between the modules is easy. Learning can be fun!

Active learning is the goal of *HandsOnPsych*. You will be engaged by hands-on activities with immediate scoring and feedback, simulations and animations that involve all the senses, self-test questions and quizzes, data-gathering experiments, video clips, and more. Each module takes 30 to 50 minutes to complete and can be done in class, in labs, in the dorm, or at home.

HandsOnPsych Contents

Module 1: Research Methods and Statistics
The Experimental Design
Statistics
Correlation
Testing

Module 2: Brain and Behaviour
Brain Cells
Neural Communication
Brain Anatomy and Function
Data Collection: Experiment on Stimulus
   Response Time
Testing

Module 3: Sensation
Psychophysics
The Ear
Smell
Touch
Testing

Module 4: Perception
Principles of Perception
Perceptual Processes
Paranormal Perception
Testing

Module 5: Learning
Habituation
Classical Conditioning

Operant Conditioning
Cognitive and Observational Learning
Testing

Module 6: Memory
The Process of Memory
Sensory Memory
Short-Term Memory
Long-Term Memory
Testing

Module 7: Consciousness
Consciousness
Sleep and Dreams
Drug Effects
Testing

Module 8: Language, Intelligence, and Problem Solving
Language
Emotional Intelligence
Problem Solving
Testing

Module 9: Development I
Introduction and Research Methods
Genetic Foundations
Prenatal Development
Testing

How to Use *HandsOnPsych*

Navigating the Modules

The 16 modules that comprise *HandsOnPsych, Version 2.0* are listed on the Module Menu page, which is accessed via the "Menu" button at the bottom left-hand corner of the screen.

Each module is self-contained. You can reach the modules from the Module Menu by clicking on each respective title. For example, clicking on Module 2, "Brain and Behaviour," will take you to the index page of that module.

On the Contents page, you will also find a link to a glossary as well as a list of sources referenced within *HandsOnPsych, Version 2.0*.

Each module begins with an index page that outlines its organization. For example, Module 2, "Brain and Behaviour," is organized into five parts: Brain Cells, Neural Communication, Brain Anatomy and Function, Data Collection: Experiment on Stimulus Response Time, and Testing. Clicking on the title of each part will take you to the beginning of that part. Each part is also divided into sections. Clicking on the title of a section will allow you to go directly to the first page of that topic.

Each page of the modules display a set of navigation buttons.

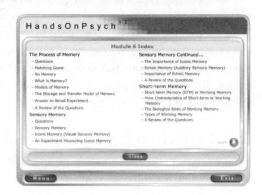

"Next" takes you to the next page of the lesson, while "Back" returns you to the previous page. The "Index" button returns you to the Contents for that particular module, while the "Menu" button returns you to the list of all the modules. Some pages display other buttons, for example, "Pop Quiz" or questions such as "Why do we have these vesicles filled with neurotransmitters?" Clicking on the question button will open a new window where you can peruse the answer and explore different learning paths. The "Close" button that appears on the last page of these learning paths closes the new window and sends you back to the page you just left.

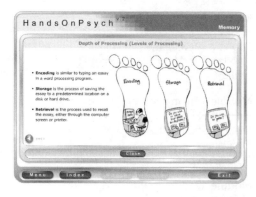

At the end of each part, you can review the questions from the first page of that part. Click on the question mark buttons to see how what you have learned in that respective module can be applied to answering these questions.

The Content

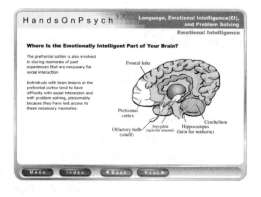

Each module is written as an interactive, multimedia lab on one of 16 topics taught in an introductory psychology classroom. Sometimes the modules deal with a topic where the content is challenging, such as biopsychology; sometimes they deal with a topic that is important but not dealt with at length in many classrooms, such as research methods and statistics. Sometimes the modules deal with a topic in an unusual way, for example, teaching hearing rather than sight in Module 3, "Sensation."

You can begin each module at the first part and proceed through to the testing component, or you can skip forward to later parts or sections if you have already completed the module and feel that you need to study one particular area more thoroughly.

Each part is organized to lead you along a learning path. Along this path you will find occasional diversions and alternate routes that delve deeper into a particular topic or bring to light an interesting fact. Once you have finished exploring, close the window and return to the main learning path.

Data Collection Experiments and Interactive Exercises

Scattered throughout each module are several data collection experiments and interactive exercises that will engage you in active learning. Follow the instructions for each one carefully. In some cases, the results of your experiments will be integrated into the lab at a subsequent point.

Testing

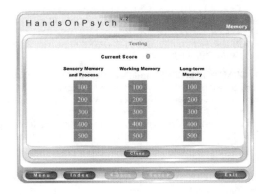

The last part of each module contain quizzes and crossword puzzles that test your understanding of the subject matter.

Each testing component contains a game show quiz. After reading the instructions, continue to the screen that shows a table with three columns of five questions each. The questions are given a value of between 100 and 500 points. Click on any of the boxes in the table and the question will appear. Select your answer and click on the arrow beside it. A cheer will let you know if you got it right, a buzzer will sound if you did not. When you have completed all of the questions, a box will appear telling you your final score and asking if you would like to retry the quiz. If you click "No" you will return to the index page for that part.

Crossword Puzzles

Each module in *HandsOnPsych, Version 2.0* contains a crossword puzzle in the testing section. These crossword puzzles will test how much you have learned from each module. There are fifteen clues for each puzzle. Print out the crossword, and see how well you can do before you check your answers.

Recommended System and Software Requirements

Operating Systems
Windows: Windows 98, Windows 2000, Windows XP
Mac OS: Mac OS X

System Requirements
IBM Compatible: Pentium 233 MHz / 64 MB RAM / 40 MB hard drive space
Mac OS: PowerPC 604e 266 MHz, G3, G4 / 64 MB RAM / 40 MB hard drive space

Sound Card and Speakers
256 colour SVGA monitor / 4X CD-ROM / Mouse

Software
Macromedia® Shockwave 8.5 (included on CD) or higher.

*Note: This product may run on computers that don't meet the recommended requirements, but performance may be slow or unstable.

Using This CD
Place CD in CD-ROM drive.
CD should auto start in 10 to 60 seconds.
Follow the on-screen instructions.

If CD does not auto start, double-click the CD icon on your computer screen (on desktop for Mac OS; under "My Computer" for Windows OS), then double-click "Start.exe."

Technical Support
If you have any questions or need technical assistance please email:
webinfo.pubcanada@pearsoned.com
Or phone: (416) 386-3413

"AS IS" LICENSE AGREEMENT AND LIMITED WARRANTY

READ THIS LICENSE CAREFULLY BEFORE OPENING THIS PACKAGE. BY OPENING THIS PACK-AGE, YOU ARE AGREEING TO THE TERMS AND CONDITIONS OF THIS LICENSE. IF YOU DO NOT AGREE, DO NOT OPEN THE PACKAGE. PROMPTLY RETURN THE UNOPENED PACKAGE AND ALL ACCOMPANYING ITEMS TO THE PLACE YOU OBTAINED THEM. *THESE TERMS APPLY TO ALL LICENSED SOFTWARE ON THE DISK EXCEPT THAT THE TERMS FOR USE OF ANY SHARE-WARE OR FREEWARE ON THE DISKETTES ARE AS SET FORTH IN THE ELECTRONIC LICENSE LOCATED ON THE DISK:*

1. GRANT OF LICENSE and OWNERSHIP: The enclosed computer programs and any data ("Software") are licensed, not sold, to you by Pearson Education Canada Inc. ("We" or the "Company") in considera-tion of your adoption of the accompanying Company textbooks and/or other materials, and your agreement to these terms. You own only the disk(s) but we and/or our licensors own the Software itself. This license allows instructors and students enrolled in the course using the Company textbook that accompanies this Software (the "Course") to use and display the enclosed copy of the Software for academic use only, so long as you com-ply with the terms of this Agreement. You may make one copy for back up only. We reserve any rights not granted to you.

2. USE RESTRICTIONS: You may <u>not</u> sell or license copies of the Software or the Documentation to oth-ers. You may <u>not</u> transfer, distribute or make available the Software or the Documentation, except to instruc-tors and students in your school who are users of the adopted Company textbook that accompanies this Software in connection with the course for which the textbook was adopted. You may <u>not</u> reverse engi-neer, disassemble, decompile, modify, adapt, translate or create derivative works based on the Software or the Documentation. You may be held legally responsible for any copying or copyright infringement which is caused by your failure to abide by the terms of these restrictions.

3. TERMINATION: This license is effective until terminated. This license will terminate automatically without notice from the Company if you fail to comply with any provisions or limitations of this license. Upon termination, you shall destroy the Documentation and all copies of the Software. All provisions of this Agreement as to limitation and disclaimer of warranties, limitation of liability, remedies or damages, and our ownership rights shall survive termination.

4. DISCLAIMER OF WARRANTY: THE COMPANY AND ITS LICENSORS MAKE <u>NO</u> WARRANTIES ABOUT THE SOFTWARE, WHICH IS PROVIDED "<u>AS-IS</u>." IF THE DISK IS DEFECTIVE IN MATE-RIALS OR WORKMANSHIP, YOUR ONLY REMEDY IS TO RETURN IT TO THE COMPANY WITHIN 30 DAYS FOR REPLACEMENT UNLESS THE COMPANY DETERMINES IN GOOD FAITH THAT THE DISK HAS BEEN MISUSED OR IMPROPERLY INSTALLED, REPAIRED, ALTERED OR DAMAGED. THE COMPANY DISCLAIMS ALL WARRANTIES, EXPRESS OR IMPLIED, INCLUDING WITHOUT LIMITATION, THE IMPLIED WARRANTIES OF MERCHANTABILITY AND FITNESS FOR A PAR-TICULAR PURPOSE. THE COMPANY DOES NOT WARRANT, GUARANTEE OR MAKE ANY REPRE-SENTATION REGARDING THE ACCURACY, RELIABILITY, CURRENTNESS, USE, OR RESULTS OF USE, OF THE SOFTWARE.

5. LIMITATION OF REMEDIES AND DAMAGES: IN NO EVENT, SHALL THE COMPANY OR ITS EMPLOYEES, AGENTS, LICENSORS OR CONTRACTORS BE LIABLE FOR ANY INCIDENTAL, INDI-RECT, SPECIAL OR CONSEQUENTIAL DAMAGES ARISING OUT OF OR IN CONNECTION WITH THIS LICENSE OR THE SOFTWARE, INCLUDING, WITHOUT LIMITATION, LOSS OF USE, LOSS OF DATA, LOSS OF INCOME OR PROFIT, OR OTHER LOSSES SUSTAINED AS A RESULT OF INJURY TO ANY PERSON, OR LOSS OF OR DAMAGE TO PROPERTY, OR CLAIMS OF THIRD PARTIES, EVEN IF THE COMPANY OR AN AUTHORIZED REPRESENTATIVE OF THE COMPANY HAS BEEN ADVISED OF THE POSSIBILITY OF SUCH DAMAGES. SOME JURISDICTIONS DO NOT ALLOW THE LIMITATION OF DAMAGES IN CERTAIN CIRCUMSTANCES, SO THE ABOVE LIMITATIONS MAY NOT ALWAYS APPLY.

6. GENERAL: THIS AGREEMENT SHALL BE CONSTRUED AND INTERPRETED ACCORDING TO THE LAWS OF THE PROVINCE OF ONTARIO. This Agreement is the complete and exclusive statement of the agreement between you and the Company and supersedes all proposals, prior agreements, oral or writ-ten, and any other communications between you and the company or any of its representatives relating to the subject matter.

Should you have any questions concerning this agreement or if you wish to contact the Company for any rea-son, please contact in writing: Editorial Manager, Pearson Education Canada, 26 Prince Andrew Place, Don Mills, Ontario, M3C 2T8.